Endangered and Threatened Animals

LEATHERBACK SEA TURTLES

by Jody Sullivan Rake

Consultant:
Robert T. Mason, PhD
Professor of Zoology
Oregon State University

CAPSTONE PRESS
a capstone imprint

Snap Books are published by Capstone Press,
1710 Roe Crest Drive, North Mankato, Minnesota 56003.
www.capstonepub.com

Library of Congress Cataloging-in-Publication Data
Rake, Jody Sullivan.
  Leatherback sea turtles / by Jody Sullivan Rake.
    p. cm. — (Snap books: endangered and threatened animals)
  Includes index.
  ISBN 978-1-4296-8584-9 (library binding)
  ISBN 978-1-62065-347-0 (ebook pdf)
  1. Leatherback turtle—Juvenile literature. 2. Sea turtles—Juvenile literature.
  I. Title.
  QL666.C546R35 2013
  597.92'89—dc23   2012006923

Editor: Brenda Haugen
Designer: Bobbie Nuytten
Media Researcher: Marcie Spence
Production Specialist: Kathy McColley

Photo Credits:
Alamy: Jack Barker, 21, Michael Patrick O'Neill, cover, Mark Conlin, 7, Scubazoo, 9 (leatherback turtle), 11
(top left), Visual&Written SL, 19, 23 (trash); Corbis: Jason Isley-Scubazoo/Science Faction, 20; iStockphoto:
MikeyLPT, 23 (turtle); NOAA, 27; SeaWorld Orlando 2011, 29; Shutterstock: amskad, 11 (top right), 17,
Andrea Danti, 9 (dolphin and whale), cozyta, 23 (trash), Demid Borodin, 23 (boat), dive-hive, 9 (green
turtle), Fanny Reno, 12, 25, grafica, design element, Heiko Kiera, 11 (bottom), Jiri Vaclavek, 8, JonMilnes,
22, Matt Jeppson, 5, 11 (middle right), Qeen, 9 (water), SerrNovik, design element, Sophia Santos, 9 (orca),
wonderisland, 23 (pollution); Visuals Unlimited: Gerald & Buff Corsi, 9 (seal), Nathan Cohen, 11 (middle left)

Printed in the United States of America in North Mankato, Minnesota.
042012   006682CGF12

Table of Contents

Chapter 1

A Leathery Loner

A female leatherback sea turtle swims close to the Mexican shore. With powerful strokes of her tough flippers, she rides the surf all the way to the beach. She has been to this beach before, when she was newly hatched from an egg. Against great odds, as a tiny turtle she found her way to the sea. The wide ocean has been her only home ever since. Now she has returned to lay her first nest of eggs.

Finding a good sandy spot, she digs a shallow hole with her back flippers. She lays about 100 delicate eggs in the hole and covers them with sand.

After burying her eggs, the turtle quietly crawls back to the surf. She will never see her young. They are entirely on their own in a big, dangerous world.

In 1980 almost 75,000 such sandy **nurseries** dotted the Mexican nesting grounds. Today there are fewer than 400.

A nest of turtle eggs in the sand

Fewer eggs mean fewer turtles. And more people are taking turtle eggs to sell for food. Leatherback sea turtles are **endangered**. Their numbers are decreasing quickly, and one day they could disappear forever.

nursery: a place for the care of young animals
endangered: at risk of dying out

Chapter 2

Unique Creatures

Leatherback sea turtles are the largest sea turtles. They are also the biggest living reptile. These sea giants grow up to 7 feet (2 meters) long. Weighing as much as 2,000 pounds (907 kilograms), leatherbacks are about as heavy as a small car. Males and females are the same size.

Leatherbacks are quite distinct from any other sea turtle. A leatherback's top shell is leathery and oily, rather than hard and bony. If you were to touch it, the top shell would feel like a baseball glove. The tough tissue on top covers loose bony **plates** underneath. The top shell has seven ridges that run from head to tail. This design helps the turtle glide through the ocean smoothly and easily.

plate: a flat, bony growth

A scientist measures a sea turtle's top shell, which is also called a carapace.

Designed for Diving

A leatherback's front flippers are long and shaped like wings. Its back flippers are short and paddle-shaped. Like other sea turtles, a leatherback can't pull its head and flippers into its shell. Its tough skin is all the protection it has.

Gentle strokes of the front flippers glide the turtle through the water. Leatherbacks are slow swimmers but deep divers. They are the deepest diving turtle, traveling to a depth of 3,900 feet (1,189 m). On one breath of air, they can stay underwater for as long as 85 minutes.

Leatherbacks wander the world's oceans to feed. They mainly eat jellyfish and **salps**. A leatherback's jaws are designed to eat soft animals. Its mouth and throat are lined with backward-pointing spines that keep its food from squirming out.

jellyfish

salp: a small, barrel-shaped, soft-bodied animal

Deep Divers

Leatherback sea turtles dive deeper than many other animals, including orcas and dolphins.

green sea turtle
360 feet (110 m)

orca
900 feet (274 m)

bottlenose dolphin
1,800 feet (549 m)

leatherback sea turtle
3,900 feet (1,189 m)

elephant seal
6,000 feet (1,829 m)

sperm whale
8,000 feet (2,438 m)

A Sandy Nest

When leatherbacks are 6 to 10 years old, they are ready to **mate**. In early winter, males and females mate at sea during their long **migrations** south. After mating, females head toward a sandy beach to lay their eggs. The shores of Mexico used to be the largest leatherback nesting ground in the world. It once contained 65 percent of all nests. Now less than 1 percent of all leatherback nests are found there. Today the largest nesting sites are found in French Guiana, Colombia, West Papua, and Indonesia.

Sea turtles come ashore to nest only at night. Digging a hole in the sand, the female lays about 100 eggs. The round, pale eggs are about the size and shape of Ping-Pong balls. The female pushes sand over the eggs with her flippers. Then she crawls back to the sea to mate again. Most females will mate and nest several times in one season. Some will lay as many as 12 nests of eggs in a season. But most of the young won't survive long enough to have young of their own.

mate: to join together for breeding
migration: the regular movement of animals as they search different places for food

Leatherback Sea Turtle Life Cycle

adult, 6-10 years

mating and laying eggs

juvenile

eggs, on beach in nest 60-65 days

hatchling

Tiny Turtles in Trouble

Buried in the sand, the eggs have some protection from **predators** and from becoming too dry. But the nest only provides so much protection. Some predators, such as seabirds, raccoons, and crabs, invade nests and eat eggs.

The remaining eggs hatch after 60 to 65 days. Just as when they were laid, the eggs hatch at night. When it is time to hatch, the tiny turtles break out of their shells. An egg tooth on a turtle's beak helps it get out of its shell. This egg tooth is temporary and will fall out in a few days. The **hatchlings** are 2 to 3 inches (5 to 7.6 cm) long.

Leatherback hatchlings are dark blue with some white along the edges and ridges of their shells.

After hatching young turtles dig their way out of the sand. Then they set out on a journey to reach the water.

It's a wonder any leatherback sea turtles make it to their first birthday. The dangers are many. Hatchlings are even more at risk. More than 90 percent of all hatchlings are eaten. Trash on the beach can slow down hatchlings or make them stop altogether.

Researchers aren't sure how baby turtles know which direction to go. The hatchlings seem to be attracted to light. The baby turtles head toward moonlight sparkling on the water. Lights from streets and buildings can confuse hatchlings. They often head toward the lights instead of the water. Those that do make it to the water must face even more predators, such as sharks and other fish.

Only about two hatchlings from every nest make it to the water. And only about one in every 1,000 leatherbacks survives long enough to become an adult. If they survive, adult leatherbacks have few predators and can live for about 30 years.

predator: an animal that hunts other animals for food
hatchling: a recently hatched animal

13

Worldwide Wanderers

Leatherback sea turtles are lone, open ocean wanderers. They spend almost their entire lives alone at sea. They come together just to mate. Only females come to shore, and that's just to lay their eggs. Leatherbacks have the widest global distribution of all reptiles. They are found in every ocean except for the icy waters of the Arctic and Antarctic. They can be found as far north as Canada and Norway. They're found as far south as New Zealand and the southern tip of Chile.

Leatherbacks are migrating animals. They make seasonal trips from cooler feeding areas in the summer to warmer nesting places in the winter. They make the longest migrations of any sea turtle, traveling about 3,700 miles (5,955 kilometers) each way.

Range and Nesting Grounds

North America

Europe

Asia

Atlantic Ocean

Pacific Ocean

Africa

Pacific Ocean

South America

Indian Ocean

Australia

N W E S

0   2000 miles
0   2000 kilometers

● Leatherback sea turtle range

● Leatherback sea turtle nesting grounds

Where Are You?

Scientists attach tracking devices to female turtles when they come ashore. Sometimes scientists can predict migratory routes based on the information they collect from the devices. People who fish can use this information. Knowing the migratory routes, anglers can move their nets out of the way and keep turtles safe.

A Vanishing Species

The population of leatherbacks is unknown. It is difficult to get a head count of these wandering ocean reptiles. Researchers usually count nesting females and determine the population from those numbers. But this is not an exact count. Many females don't always nest at the same beaches.

Scientists believe that most leatherbacks live in the Atlantic Ocean. In 1982 researchers estimated that about 115,000 nesting females lived there. More than half of them could be found in Mexico. In 1996 the population was estimated to be as few as 20,000. It had dropped to less than 20 percent of what it had been only 14 years earlier. Some populations are nearly gone. The Malaysian leatherback population has dropped from 10,155 nests counted in 1956 to just 37 in 1995.

The **species** is in serious trouble. People and natural predators have caused the leatherbacks' decline. But people are also working to stop it.

species: a group of animals or plants that share common characteristics

Researchers are trying to find ways to help the sea turtle population grow.

Nesting Females in Costa Rica

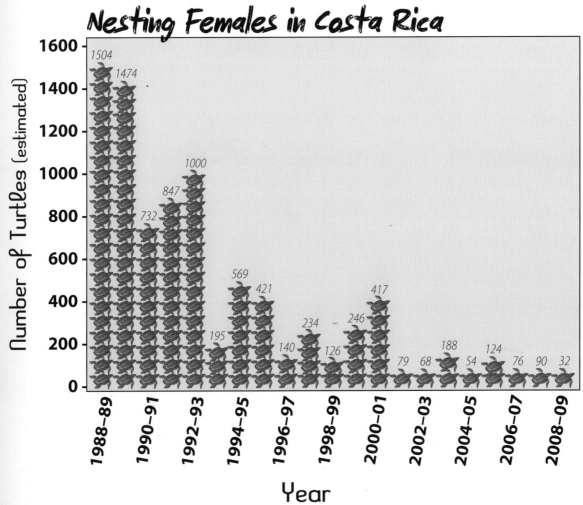

Number of Turtles (estimated)

1600 · 1400 · 1200 · 1000 · 800 · 600 · 400 · 200 · 0

1504 · 1474 · 732 · 847 · 1000 · 195 · 569 · 421 · 140 · 234 · 126 · 246 · 417 · 79 · 68 · 188 · 54 · 124 · 76 · 90 · 32

1988–89 · 1990–91 · 1992–93 · 1994–95 · 1996–97 · 1998–99 · 2000–01 · 2002–03 · 2004–05 · 2006–07 · 2008–09

Year

Chapter 4

A Sea of Trouble

Leatherback sea turtles are endangered throughout the world. In some places they are almost gone. Many reasons have led to the decline of leatherbacks. But the two main threats are fishing nets and **poaching**.

Every year fishermen throw thousands of lines and nets into the sea. But along with fish and shrimp, they also catch sea turtles. The turtles are scooped up and can't find their way out of the tightly woven nets. Sometimes turtles get tangled up in the nets and can't break free. Because these nets are often dragged behind boats for hours, the trapped turtles usually end up drowning. Other types of fishing gear can cause serious injury and death to sea turtles. Hooks poke and tear the turtles' heads and flippers. Fishing lines wrap around flippers and cause deep cuts.

poaching: hunting or fishing illegally

A fishing net on a reef catches a leatherback sea turtle.

Nest Raiders

Leatherbacks don't just face threats at sea. Although leatherbacks are a protected species, they are still the victims of poaching. Everywhere leatherbacks go to lay their eggs, they are in danger. Poachers wait on the beach for nesting females to lay eggs. Then the poachers take the eggs to sell for food. In some areas more than 95 percent of leatherback eggs have been illegally harvested. Poachers also take the adult females and sell them for their meat and oily shells. In Papua, New Guinea, people take oil from turtles' hides and use it for lotions and oil lamps.

Poachers try to catch a sea turtle.

Protecting Nests

As in other parts of the world, nesting leatherbacks in Costa Rica, once plentiful, were nearly gone. In the 1980s, there were more than 200 females. By 1997 there were fewer than 10 females. In 1995 the Leatherback Trust helped establish Las Baulas National Park to protect turtle eggs and hatchlings. Workers place screens around nests to protect them from predators. They stand guard to protect the nests from poachers. Often workers remove eggs and take them to a safe hatchery. This action protects the eggs from being washed out to sea at high tide. Hatchery nests are located higher on the beach and are dug by hand to match the natural nests. In January 2010 24 tagged females returned, along with 15 untagged females, which were new arrivals. That season produced 346 hatchlings. These results show that conservation efforts are working.

Many other serious threats kill leatherbacks each year. Trash carelessly tossed in the ocean or even on beaches is harmful to sea turtles. The turtles sometimes mistake plastic bags for jellyfish. Just one plastic bag can cause a deadly blockage in a sea turtle's stomach or intestines.

Pollution from factories, oil drilling, boats, and marinas gushes into the ocean. This waste poisons sea turtles and causes defects in their young. Oil spills, such as the one in the Gulf of Mexico in 2010, are serious threats to leatherbacks. When turtles come to the surface to breathe, the oil can plug their noses.

A plastic bag creates a hazard for turtles in the ocean.

Beaches changed or destroyed by construction have reduced nesting areas to a fraction of what they once were. Large numbers of beach tourists and beach activities also bother turtles and their nesting **habitats**.

Threats to the Leatherback Sea Turtle

BOAT STRIKES

FISHING NETS

POLLUTION

PREDATORS OF EGGS AND HATCHLINGS

EATING TRASH

habitat: the natural place and conditions in which an animal or plant lives

Chapter 5

To the Rescue

Many groups and individuals have joined forces to save leatherback sea turtles. Government agencies and nongovernment organizations alike are committed to protecting leatherbacks.

Leatherback sea turtles are protected by the Endangered Species Act (ESA). The ESA was signed into law in 1973. All species listed in the ESA are protected. Killing them or taking their eggs is against the law. Leatherbacks are listed as critically endangered by the International Union for Conservation of Nature and Natural Resources (IUCN). This means they could become extinct. The designation also means they receive extra protection, such as tough laws against poaching, to keep them from going extinct. Those breaking the law could go to prison for a year and pay a fine of up to $50,000.

A female retuns to the ocean after laying her eggs.

Leatherbacks are also listed in an international treaty known as CITES. The treaty is an agreement among the countries that have leatherback sea turtles. The treaty makes it illegal to sell or transport leatherback sea turtles. It is also illegal to sell or transport their eggs or any parts of their bodies. But even though there are tough laws against harming sea turtles and their eggs, poaching continues.

The National Marine Fisheries Service (NMFS) has designated most leatherback nesting beaches as critical habitat. This ruling means that the area is necessary for the survival of individuals and the species. It provides another layer of protection for the turtles. People are not allowed to enter or disturb these areas.

You Can Help

The list of conservation organizations that help leatherbacks is a long one. The Sierra Club and the World Wildlife Fund are longtime champions of all **threatened** animals. The Sea Turtle Conservancy has been working to save all sea turtles since 1959.

The Leatherback Trust is one of the largest organizations dedicated to saving leatherback sea turtles. It works with many countries to protect nesting areas. It educates the public about leatherbacks and the threats they face. The trust established the Las Baulas Project, an effort to protect leatherback nesting sites in Costa Rica.

The results of the conservation efforts are mixed. Some populations are slowly recovering. Others continue to decline. But the good news is that the conservation process is still pretty new. Most conservation efforts didn't really get started until the 1980s or 1990s. It will take years of work to save leatherback sea turtles. With more work, the animals can be saved.

TED

The U.S. government worked with fishermen to develop the turtle **excluder** device, or TED. TEDs are metal trap doors placed in the middle of fishing nets. Small animals such as shrimp pass through the bars of the TED and are caught in the net bag. When turtles are scooped into the net, they run into the bars, causing the trap door to open. The turtle is able to swim right out. This device has saved thousands of sea turtles.

A turtle escapes a net through a trap door.

threatened: in danger of dying out
excluder: a device designed to keep something out

What Can I Do?

Do you think you're too young to help save leatherbacks? You're not. The first thing you should do is learn all you can about leatherbacks. Then you can teach others what you've learned. Here are more things you can do:

- Start a Save the Leatherbacks club at school. Make posters and give classroom talks.
- Have a Save the Leatherback bake sale, read-a-thon, or other fund-raiser. Donate the money you raise to a sea turtle hospital or organization.
- Keep turtle nesting grounds clean. Reuse and recycle paper, plastic, and glass. Throw away trash in a trash can. If you live near the ocean, organize or join in a beach clean-up.
- Get inspired. Visit the Leatherback Trust website and read the incredible story of how kids like you are making a difference.

Casey Sokolovic

Do you think one person can't make a difference? Meet Casey Sokolovic from Winterville, North Carolina.

Casey's passion for sea turtles began after a third grade field trip. She visited the Karen Beasley Sea Turtle Rescue and Rehabilitation Center on Topsail Island, North Carolina. Casey was inspired by the work of the center, which rehabilitates turtles and releases them back to the wild.

In 2006 Casey started her own education and awareness program, Help Them L.A.S.T. (Love A Sea Turtle). She also has raised funds to help sea turtles. She sold cookies and donated the sales to the Topsail Island sea turtle hospital. She inspired a Fair Trade coffee with coffee company Joe Van Gogh. The company donates 10 percent of its profits to the sea turtle hospital.

After the Gulf of Mexico oil spill in 2010, Casey created another charity, The Great Bake for Oceans' Sake. It is a coast-to-coast effort to encourage people to organize fund-raising bake sales to benefit ocean conservation groups.

Casey helps at the Sea Turtle Hospital and speaks to student groups. She has made an educational DVD. In 2011 Casey was the winner of the SeaWorld/Busch Gardens Environmental Excellence Award for her efforts. After winning the award, Casey said in interviews, "My expectations are simple and straightforward: get outside, learn while having fun, and inspire youth activism. One person can make a difference!"

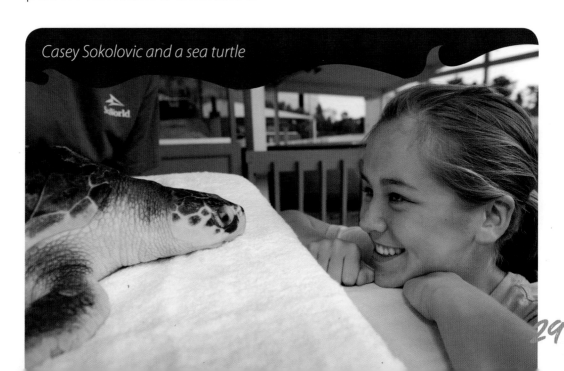

Casey Sokolovic and a sea turtle

Glossary

endangered (in-DAYN-juhrd)—at risk of dying out

excluder (iks-KLOO-dur)—a device designed to keep something out

habitat (HAB-uh-tat)—the natural place and conditions in which an animal or plant lives

hatchling (HACH-ling)—a recently hatched animal

mate (MATE)—to join together for breeding

migration (mye-GRAY-shuhn)—the regular movement of animals as they search different places for food

nursery (NUR-sur-ee)—a place for the care of young animals

plate (PLAYT)—a flat, bony growth

poaching (POHCH-ing)—hunting or fishing illegally

predator (PRED-uh-tur)—an animal that hunts other animals for food

salp (SALP)—a small, barrel-shaped, soft-bodied animal

species (SPEE-sheez)—a group of animals or plants that share common characteristics

threatened (THRET-uhnd)—in danger of dying out

Read More

Allen, Kathy. *Sea Turtles' Race to the Sea: A Cause and Effect Investigation*. Animals on the Edge. Mankato, Minn.: Capstone Press, 2011.

Hinman, Bonnie. *Threat to the Leatherback Turtle*. On the Verge of Extinction. Hockessin, Del.: Mitchell Lane Publishers, 2009.

Hoare, Ben, and Tom Jackson. *Endangered Animals*. DK Eyewitness Books. New York: DK Pub., 2010.

Internet Sites

FactHound offers a safe, fun way to find Internet sites related to this book. All of the sites on FactHound have been researched by our staff.

Here's all you do:

Visit *www.facthound.com*

Type in this code: 9781429685849

Super-cool stuff!   Check out projects, games and lots more at **www.capstonekids.com**

Index